Only So Many Autumns

Only So Many Autumns

Betsy Joseph

LITERARY PRESS
LAMAR UNIVERSITY

ISBN: 978-1-942956-69-3
Library of Congress Control Number: 2019944112

Manufactured in the United States

Lamar University Literary Press
Beaumont, Texas

My gratitude
to those I have loved and lost
as well as to those whose presence remains strong in my life.

You know who you are.

Recent Poetry from Lamar University Literary Press

For information on these and other Lamar University Literary Press books
go to www.Lamar.edu/literarypress

Acknowledgments

The author gratefully acknowledges the following journals in which some of these poems appeared.

Texas Poetry Calendar 2017
Texas Poetry Calendar 2019
Ocotillo Review
Voices from Within

Salutations

In the silvery half-light of early Texas mornings,
when calico cats skitter across dew-topped grass
much as dragonflies skim late August lakes;
at the hour when children still slumber to misty kayak dreams,
so deeply they smile and breathe;
in the absolute quiet when the cicadas' drone
has grown softer and intermittent
and a slight breeze ruffles the languid ferns,
this is the time I rise and offer salutations to the world.

CONTENTS

Miscellany

Haiku Collection

Cinquain Collection

Pantoum Collection

Sonnet Collection

Tributes

Family

Roots and Wings

They provided her with deep abiding roots
this New England artist and West Texas dreamer.
The roots dug deep, nestled down for stability
while still allowing certain yielding
when her desire arose to venture forth.
She could not have asked for better grounding,
and she always knew she was well nourished
by these two who harked from such different places
but who blended so beautifully.

They also provided her with wings
so she could launch herself when it was her time.
The artist-mother and journalist-father
gave her room to fly while keeping her in sight
and also keeping their judgments few.
She soared, determined to make wise choices,
grateful for the ones that proved their worth,
pushing back others that did not serve.
During times of tumult,
watchful eyes worried, gentle voices soothed.
They trusted her strength.

In time her providers of roots and wings
grew smaller and weaker
until they were but a speck in the light
before they flickered and died.
They had nurtured the deep abiding roots
which continued to ground her.
They also had fashioned their daughter with lasting wings
to lift and carry her for the remainder of her time.

Skipping Stones

I learned to skip stones alongside a chilly river
in southeastern Colorado.
I was seven that summer
with two brothers taking turns to demonstrate the form:
index finger crooked around the edge of a nice flat stone,
middle finger on the other side;
wrist bent back and then a quick snap forward,
angling the stone against the water's smooth surface.
My own errant attempts tended to bounce and sink.

My brothers, though, in evident spirited competition,
skimmed carefully selected stones
some smooth, others rippled
and with practiced grace their stones skipped and skiffed,
each brother counting the times his lucky stone
would glance off the counter-clockwise spin—
a contest that could last for hours.

I observed and imitated
and occasionally got it right,
but mostly I squatted in the presence of masters,
in awe of their post-adolescent confidence and skill
and I was content.

For Frivolous Reasons

Those long treks from Texas to Connecticut
to visit Mom's family took three long days
punctuated by routine stops—
gas and restroom breaks, picnics at roadside parks—
until arriving, at last,
at some nondescript motor court to unwind and sleep.
Only to repeat the sequence the following morning.
Early. At five a.m. Dad had his mission.
And we never stopped for frivolous reasons.

Mom was a trooper, keeping Dad caffeinated
via a tall thermos by her leg while also keeping peace
among three mostly bored and squirmy children
sandwiched tightly in the backseat.
I was always in the middle.

The point is, Dad did not want to tarry longer
than need be unless it was his idea.
I do not begrudge the side trips to Civil War battle sites
in the great states of Mississippi, Tennessee, and Virginia.
They were a grand history lesson, and definitely not frivolous.

The point, though, is about balance.
Traveling through Lancaster, PA one hot day,
Mom provided a lesson of her own.
She gazed longingly at Amish quilts for sale,
drawn to the bright geometry draped over clotheslines,
and touched Dad gently. Could we, she asked him,
stop for a few minutes—just a few?
But Dad had his mission.

From my vantage point, it seemed Dad never deliberated
but drove, if not accelerated, past the blur of lovely quilts,
my mother straining to look while she could.
The response, if Dad provided one, was probably
something about not stopping for frivolous reasons.

All these years later, I know I am
a planner, an echo of my Dad.
But Mom was not the only one
who longed and strained to see
the rhythms in those Amish quilts.
So I will stop for frivolous reasons.

Upon Having No Marbles
A Young Sister's Lament

Never underestimate the grit of a six year old sister.
Bent on playing marbles with brothers but having none—
marbles, that is; the brothers are here to stay—
she pleads dramatically with her mother
for a ride to the nearby Five and Dime.
Six year olds, unlike mothers, though,
are not in the middle of some important household task.
Six year olds are single minded and can be relentless in their demands.

Once home with marbles in hand—
the prettiest this young sister could select, the colors kaleidoscopic—
she bounces into the room, boldly triumphant.
It is empty, however, and bereft of brothers.
The mesh bag remains clutched in hands now sweaty and clenched
in a room once rowdy-turned still.

The brothers, it turns out, had tired of marbles,
and moved on next door for a long game of Risk;
her mother, of course, resumed her interrupted chores.
The sister sighs deeply, disappointed and deflated.
The day has not turned out as she planned.
Slowly she releases her marbles from the bag,
a scatter of colors pinging on the hardwood floor.

The Last Firefly of Summer

This late October evening
I sit with my oldest brother on the long narrow porch
of a ranch in the Texas Hill Country.

No longer in the midst of our youth,
we are more settled in our reflections
and even the shared silence is companionable.

The sky now gone almost tar-pitch black—
no light pollution to speak of—
a sudden pinprick of bright
startles us from our reverie and reminiscing.
It is like a beacon pulling us back into childhood.

"The last firefly of summer," one of us comments
as the firefly continues to blink on and off
for several minutes to the chorus of cicadas.

I rock and drift, wondering for a moment
if we would see any fireflies together again,
aware that time is not slowing its pace for us
and we are pitching forward into more fragile years.

Then I glance at my sibling in profile,
and in the soft golden glow of the porch light
he is once again the nonchalant adolescent brother
who sometimes let me perch, my seating a bit wobbly,
on the sturdy handlebars of his bike
while he pedaled madly down the sidewalk
and excited terror filled my chest.

West Texas Annie

By the time I knew her
my grandmother was ample-bodied,
and her steel blue-gray eyes gazed
upon the world through wire rimmed glasses.

Of Scots-Irish descent, she claimed to possess
the special gift of second sight,
predicting her grandchildren's comings
before the announcements were made.
No one dared challenge her.

Hard scrabbling was the only way of life she knew,
preparing pinto beans three times daily
during the wasteland years of the Thirties,
grateful for the availability of the those brown-speckled legumes.
That my father continued to enjoy them the remainder of his life
was long a mystery to my brothers and me.
We figured he would not want to eat another pinto bean
once he departed that limiting landscape.
We did not understand his gratitude.

All we knew was that Grandma's tongue and tone could be sharp
and her hugs and smiles were few.
It took years before I considered her rough passages
and fully comprehended the many adversities
that molded the whole of her life.

When on one visit she surprised me with several dresses
fashioned and sewn for my doll,
all from remnants of her own clothing,
I came to realize she knew little girls better than I thought.

Wife and Blackberries Waiting

At twenty-six my mother found herself
perched, unexpectedly, atop a large suitcase
under the only tree in the front yard.
It protected her from the intense Texas August sun.
The evicted possessions belonging to her and my father
huddled about her as if equally startled
to find themselves without a home.
Along with my mother they waited for my father to arrive.

Dallas was not prepared for the influx of returning GIs,
so many at the same time and without enough places to live,
and arrangements were made hastily and often covertly.
In my parents' case the issue was an apartment
sublet without the landlord's knowledge or consent.
Word leaked out, the landlord reacted,
and my mother opened the door one day to an eviction notice.
Effective immediately.
While waiting for my father to arrive with a solution, she hoped,
and as the heat continued to blaze,
she reflexively rubbed her belly,
a belly ripening for an early October birth: my oldest brother.

Also reaching fullness in various parts of Texas,
blackberries were growing plump, nearing their second harvest.
While they enjoyed the heat, my mother clearly did not.
Had she been thinking of blackberries, she might have longed
for their juicy sweetness, a brief refreshment from the heat.
She might also have longed for her family back East,
feeling a tug of homesickness for all she left behind
when she met a Navy man three years earlier,
quite handsome in his officer's uniform, and married him.
Mostly what she longed for was my father's arrival home.

And so my mother continued to wait.
My father finally arrived with cobbled arrangements
to stay with friends who then helped
my parents find a more suitable place.

And so my mother nested and waited,
in sync with blackberry bushes also ripe and full,
all readying to produce their fruit.

Pastel Poems

There is a poem
in the way my son follows his Nana's teaching—
how the barn, though in the foreground,
should be drawn to scale,
how to use fingers to blend
the mountains into the sky,
how to identify the firs by shape
to avoid unnecessary detail.

Her practiced eyes,
although growing dim,
hold in their collective memory
all the lessons and applications
that help to guide my son's hand
to create the landscape in pastel.

His cousin works beside him,
brows furrowed in concentration
as he gazes upon the same scene
from his position in the field.
He too listens to Nana,
working the images before him
onto the coarse white pad.

When finished,
the boys compare their efforts to Nana's
pointing out the deficiencies in their own.
The rest of us
see two poems in pastel—
both efforts reflective and unique—
and the satisfied smile of the artist
who oversaw them.

My Father's Wisdom

When he was alive my father would unfurl wisdom
like the thin pine curls that blanketed his workshop floor
while he labored on a project.
His words would unroll and I would take them slowly,
laying them edge to edge to stretch the full import
of their worth.

Yellow curls of pine, laid edge to edge,
with the answer somewhere in between.

What If

What if I had said no all those years ago
and traded chalk for a trowel and pick,
leaving all that I had known
for desert lands so far away?

Would you have bestowed your blessing,
wished me well and safe,
would you have continued to love me
that day and the next?

Would you have dwelled on potential adventures
rather than possible dangers,
would you have gazed past your paternal control,
could you have realized I was simply reaching
for my dream and not for yours?

If I had just had your blessing
I could have understood your fear—
the reluctance to release your youngest
and a girl child at that—
and perhaps eased you through that journey.

But those were not the terms,
and a blessing not bestowed
cannot be accepted.
Moreover, I was not brave enough
to leave in the wake of your disappointment.

So I remained,
but that did not necessarily keep me safe and sound.
There are always other perils even close to home.
I put aside the idea of trowel and pick
and chalk became my tool of trade,
serving me well for decades.
I have no regrets.

Except for that one conversation
when you told me I was meant for one destiny

yet my heart yearned for another.
I wanted to be right that time.

The Essence of Wood

Before my father lost two fingers to an eager saw
that leapt at his impatience
(so preoccupied was he with his grandson's 13th birthday),
he would often carve and whittle objects
from unimaginative blocks of wood.

Someone in our family has the chipmunk
he fashioned one summer in Cuchara,
the spoon valley that gazes up at K-T Mountain
and nestles in the lap of southeastern Colorado.

His lovely carving of a slender beauty
bending forward to wash her hair
(or pull it out—I've never been quite sure which)
graces a table in my own home,
her femininity both vulnerable and strong.

His earlier pieces were less sophisticated,
chunky almost in dimension and shape,
and without great attention to detail.
But in time his fingers became more nimble,
and the forms he rendered seemed to reflect
a mellowing, a slowing down
as if the process itself had acquired new meaning and respect.

I was going to say, on this topic of whittling,
that everything seems all wrong now,
that Time, a sage craftsman, has become the whittler,
that it is he, in fact, who holds my father's form in hand
and shaves—ever so gingerly—
the layers of his fruitful life:
his dimension and his shape,
bringing a substantial man closer to a raw block of wood.

Though saddened, I am not completely fooled
for my father taught me early that character remains in the wood.

Words and Wood
Father's Day 2006

A life that could have been linear and barren
as the Texas scrub brush landscape that had birthed him,
resonates instead with fullness and contribution.

My father,
who fashioned his life with words and wood
in a world of twists and turns,
has left marvels in sawdust script,
creations born of determination and grit.
His life reveals histories through his writing
and shines from the varnished wood grains
of the furniture made smooth by his hands.

Words and wood:
Enduring elements to those who love him.

At War with the Pathogens

On this night in the emergency room
my father is at war with the pathogens,
mustering both courage and resolve
to do battle in this sterile place
against an enemy he cannot see.

Those who attend him in this state
subscribe to trench warfare tactics
that bear little resemblance to those familiar
to this Texan during the Second World War.
Probing hands, pricking needles,
commands to lie, sit, stand—
all remind him that he is not in charge.

Still it is his war.
It is his body.
It is his will
that will choose whether to win or lose the fight.

The enemy, however, underestimates my father
whose gaunt frame attests to months of illness.
This silent host has not anticipated
a counter-charge from this weakened soldier
whose rallying west Texas grit
is the most effective weapon of all.

First Keeper of My Heart

"Let me whisper you into the land of ease,"
I offered while smoothing my dad's bald head
and rubbing the hand that once typed
volumes of newsworthy words.

Morphine-dulled eyes gazed into mine,
a half-smile forming on lips chapped and tired
from answering questions that his brain
could no longer grasp.

So little time, so much to say—for both of us.
All I could leave him, the only peace to ease his end
was a daughter's assurance that his wife,
his heart mate of sixty-six years,
would be loved and cared for when he was gone.

And then his hand brought mine to his lips
and his brown eyes fixed onto my own.
Staring beyond me, he squeezed my fingers,
and I lay my head upon the quivering chest
of the first keeper of my heart.

A Blend of Tea and Artistry
Mother's Day 2006

This is my mother:
bold brush strokes of oil on canvas,
light sweep of pastels on paper—
portraits and still lifes her preference of expression.

This is also my mother:
gourmet cook and talented seamstress,
patient nurturer who saved scraps of biscuit dough
for me to fashion my own designs.

This is my mother, too:
a ready companion for an afternoon break
of cinnamon toast and tea
on the raw winter afternoons of my adolescence.

Just the two of us.
With perhaps our cat.
But never my brothers.

Cuchara Memories Revisited

The we of then and the we of now—
who are these people whose voices
have become echoes off mountain walls?

We search for our ghosts in the spoon valley of memory
along the rocky trails,
in the tiny village
where remains of ourselves wait for rediscovery.

Even the younger ones,
teenagers and young men now,
recall the children they once were in those places
but finding them gone now in the bittersweet blur of time,
they see instead the evolution of self
through family ties.

Now when we gather together
we create a different whole:
forming circles of us everywhere,
rolling like the stream
toward some infinite point in nature—
winding and side-stepping our course
but for now unbroken in the continuum of memory—
voices reverberating from the stones,
ghost shadows watching from the ridge.

The Shadows and the Shallows

My father entered the shadows first,
leaving my mother on the periphery
like a frightened swan longing for her missing mate.

The explanations
and then the reminders
did not come easily.
My mother mourned daily
and awaited my father's return.

I would look into her dark brown eyes,
eyes so much like my own;
I would hold her hand, gnarled yet soft,
and watch her silent keening

until my heart, too, began to break, my resolve to crumble.
My murmurs became inaudible and dry,
soon sifting like silt around me.

And then, as though she heard a noise,
my mother forgot her deafness and followed the sound
that did not reach my ears, nor did my eyes
sight the movement that must have beckoned her to follow.

No longer on the border,
my mother herself retreated into the darkness,
with her figure cutting a long shadow
before me in the weak afternoon sun.

Not yet, but soon perhaps—and if I strain to listen—
I hope to hear the rustle of wings and the delicate splash
of two wonders in the shallow marshes
readying for their last migration, joining in a V formation,
together again once more.

Loving You Still and in Spite of
A Daughter's Tale

I watched the tapestries of your selves unthread,
filaments slender and fragile,
the patterns of your lives becoming less distinct.

I sat between you, a hand on each knee,
lightly squeezing as you struggled to find
me in the unraveling, amidst those loose threads.

I ached to be a weaver, to sit before a loom
and repair the loss, to halt the advance of your nemesis
who in mincing steps was leading you away,
from us and even from each other.

Loving you still and in spite of that cunning thief,
I continued to look for you in your hands
known so long and well, in smiles
that became more rare, in the photographs
that adorned your dresser.

Now as time softens your passings, I remember less
the unraveling and more the richness of your
tapestried lives;
I long so to enfold myself in those threads—
inhaling memories, absorbing images—
twirling as I find you both again.

When Small Recognitions Are Enough

I am dear to you in some way.
I know this because you anxiously search my face,
your hands limp in your lap.
Your gaze rests on my eyes
and a flicker relays the glint of recognition
before the light suddenly expires,
the familiar dullness in your stare speaking
what my heart does not want to hear.
Dementia, demon bastard, wins yet another round.

I raise your ninety-one year old hands to my lips.
It is no matter, I tell myself.
I am dear to you in some way,
and sometimes the small recognitions have to be enough.

Dallas Christmas 2012

Bittersweet was my mother's last Christmas,
all the more since we did not know
she would leave us six weeks later.

It was a Sunday morning, my brother and I
among the very few visitors on the Memory Care floor.
Snow was falling in large gentle flakes
and drifting lazily from clouds the shade of slate,
the window view seeming more riveting, the room less empty.
I thought of people sitting in churches everywhere
listening to the age-old story of Mary giving birth,
realizing the speechless awe she must have felt
as her womb produced a son.
Then I looked at our mother—
not a Mary but a Madgie—
not in Bethlehem but in Texas—
because this Connecticut girl long ago married a McCamey boy—
and I wondered, as her eyes flickered momentarily
between my brother and me,
if she still possessed some memory of birthing us.
We each stroked a deeply veined hand,
murmuring expressions of love
while she stared ahead, gaze locked on something—
a caregiver moving across the floor?
a lit, decorated tree in the corner?
the snow continuing softly in the deepening winter light?
Such a random question: wondering if she recalled
giving birth to my brothers and me.
What did it matter?
Small and delicate between the two of us,
she still represented the life force and we,
we were the bookends holding *her* in place,
paying tribute to all motherhood
that silvery Christmas Day.

Dance Memories

Yesterday afternoon, February dreary,
I danced with my mother's hands
to Glenn Miller's "In the Mood,"
her feet resting on the floor
mine tapping the rhythm she could no longer hear.

Putting my mouth to her ear I asked,
"Remember, Mom? Remember dancing with Dad?
This was one of your favorite songs."

Her eyelids fluttered once, twice,
and in those movements I imagined
my father sweeping her across the floor
of a New York dance club when Big Band was king.
Her dark hair rested against his blond,
and they swirled as if the moment might never end.
It lasted sixty-six years.

"Go dance with Dad again," I murmured.
"He's out there waiting, waiting just for you."
My mother nodded—I think she nodded—
as the last note rose and fell
and her gaze became blank once again.
I then tapped my way through "Chattanooga Choo-Choo,"
this time by myself.

From My Mother's Voice

I lived with a man for sixty-six years,
an earnest man with west Texas roots,
and one day he disappeared.
I looked for him behind me.
I looked for him in corners.
I looked for him in bed where he would spoon
and wrap his weakened arms around me.

I wanted him to appear, to share a table with me,
to touch my face, touch our hands.

Instead, a familiar stranger would come,
rub my hands and arms with lavender lotion,
murmur unintelligible sounds that soothed and calmed me.
Her dark doe eyes looked much like my husband's,
and I would stare into them until she slipped away
to return some other time.

I lived with a man for sixty-six years
and one day he disappeared.
At long last I decided to find him.
I pulled at the air as if it were a veil,
as if he were standing behind it
in the gauze of pale light,
in the lingering scent of lavender.

Mother to Sons

It seems that I hold steady
so that you can move,
and all the while I watch you
from not so very far away
as you chart your way in life.

It is not so much a sacrifice
as it is an intrigue,
and I marvel at my constancy
(and your wild aberrations)
realizing that it is this combination
that keeps us all on course.

Still, it is tough to be a compass
for someone else.
I know sometimes I err
in my calculations,
sending warnings about a wind
that brings no harm
or trusting a calm sea
when turbulence lies ahead.

You will forgive these misjudgments
just as I will continue my vigil on the shore,
staying steady and strong
so that you may move.

Those Saturday Evenings

Saturday evenings without your dad
came to mean ice cream—
the best kind with hot fudge, nuts,
and always a cherry.

One bottle of cherries:
Such a small, small price for giggling
and snuggling on the couch
so accustomed to our body dents.

I could not provide much more—
certainly not all the answers—
but I could promise chocolate sundaes
on nights dark and cold
in the house I fought to keep our own.

For those hours
life's cares retreated to the shadows
and we prospered on the comfort of hot fudge
and the closeness of us.

Innocence and Experience

At five
my son worried about dying
and was curious about heaven.
If wishes could be granted,
he would have all of us
(including the cats)
make the starry journey together
holding hands (and paws)
to ensure we did not drift apart.
It was a lovely thought, I told him,
and I wondered how long
he could be comforted by that image.

Now
he is almost ten
and his questions no longer center
on death and the hereafter.
He worries instead about life after divorce.
His brows furrow
when his dad does not come home.
He searches my vacant eyes for comprehension
and, finding none,
drifts into troubled sleep.

Sometimes
he cries out in the night and I go to his side,
gently rub his back,
and bring his outstretched arm back under the cover.
He doesn't seem to remember these occasions
but I cannot forget them.
I consider asking
if he is reaching for hands (and paws)
in an effort to keep us all together.
But then I don't need to ask.
I already know.

Poems in the Process of Creation

You are poems in the process of creation,
organic wonders taking form,
defining boundaries—
defying them as well—
pondering still the possibilities.

I might think to mold you,
identify your niche.
It is easy to close my eyes
and contemplate my mark
on your existence.

Such is not to be.
Others before me
have pointed out the futility
of speculation;
they much prefer the element of surprise.

I can imagine the sonnets, the ballads,
the free verse forthcoming;
I might even guess that a limerick or two
could be fashioning as you develop.

I celebrate your beings
as I watch you on your way,
and I think I am also a poem
but in the process of revision.
I celebrate that, too.

This Crimson Rose

This crimson rose
that lies wrapped in wet paper towel
along the counter in uncertain repose,
this crimson rose
will not go anywhere tonight.

Destined for a young girl's heart,
its fragrance fills our kitchen
even hours later
as I enter for something to drink.
Standing at the darkened window
I recall my son's self-conscious smile
when asking if he could cut
the newest bloom from the bush.

Then he spent the evening
waiting for the call that never came,
watching Rangers baseball
while also glancing at the clock.
He desperately tried to appear nonchalant.
The rest of us pretended it didn't matter either.

He graduates tomorrow
summa cum laude
so certain of his college goals,
equally baffled by matters of the heart.

Reconfigurations

What are reconfigurations for
if not to change around in size and form?
We are puzzle pieces,
these people I know as family,
and we become different pictures with each new arrangement
that comes into play.

The oldest son leaves the nest
venturing to the university in Austin,
and we rotate round the table
in musical chairs fashion.
One of us finds a new spot when the music stops.
New puzzle picture.

The bedroom kept intact
becomes the most silent of museums.
Memorabilia on the walls
whisper tales of a young boy's life and deeds.
In the darkness, the room does not smell of him now.
He will return to it, slumbering deeply with his six foot frame.
The patterns are all shifting,
forming swirls and whorls across our lives.
I peel memories like old strips of wallpaper,
contemplating the new design that will take its place,
awaiting a configuration different from the others
when it is his brother's turn to leave.

Observations on My Younger Son

On this late spring day
I observe your silhouette and note your pose,
languid and unassuming,
your shoulder blade singular and unique.

You twirl a blade of grass between two fingers:
holding it first to catch its translucence,
then releasing it so that it floats unhurriedly to your knee.
In the warming clarity of sunlight
you become that blade of grass—
individual, singular, unique.
There is absolutely no one like you
in the vast prairie of humanity
whose contributions equal yours
when your energy is unfurled.

Love

The Deliberateness of Love

The deliberateness of love is stalwart
in the presence of doubt,
throws a cloak over the specter of confusion,
and will volunteer for missions on the front line.

It is never hesitant or craven
but neither does it seek the spotlight
to declare its intentions.

It is quite satisfied to await the nocturnal shadows
and intone the syllables of the heart.

Love and Bone China

This night I think of my grandmother's practiced words
as she sat at her table with its oilcloth cover,
pieces of dishware laid out before her.
"Bone china" she called it—
my young self fascinated and questioning,
"Whose bones?" as I pondered the set.
She would smile and say, "Bone china means company best."
I still wondered whose bones made up those cups and plates.

Flanked by white glue and Q-tips she would begin,
with patient and painstaking care,
to repair hairline cracks and reinforce seams
or, in some cases, perform surgery
by assembling fragments as if studying a puzzle.

She never seemed to do this with the everyday china,
West Texas sturdy and plain.
Now I understand why.
These pieces carried their chips and nicks with casual aloofness,
accustomed as they were to daily contact with tumbleweed
and flatland, with hands callous and careless.
They were hardy, serviceable,
reliable features of my childhood.

Later I came to discover that love—
much like my grandmother's bone china—
is fragile,
lacking sagebrush robustness
and not always withstanding even gentle pressure well.
Too many hairline cracks and it will SNAP—
the paper-thin shards delicate,
trying to become whole again under quivering fingers,
while wondering just how long the glue will hold.

Present Tenses

Come unto me
in the twilight of the evening
and we will speak in present tenses;
you will announce yourself
my bird of paradise,
and we will feast on pomegranates
that reflect the dying amber sun.

I will leave you then
hushed and still,
nestled somewhere between night and dawn
with the remnant seeds cupped in a palm
strangely protective;
the tremor in your wing
brushed softly by my leaving
will be my tremor also,
and the restless sigh will echo mine—
but we only spoke in present tenses
and tomorrow is on the rise.

Perhaps Some Gentle Morn

I tuck myself into your side,
under your wingspan that reaches wider than I deserve.
My head leans into your neck
and I listen to your heartbeat:
steady, strong, and sure.

I am your softness and your strength,
and I will ready my nest
for your comings and goings—
sad upon your leaving but secure in your return.

Perhaps some gentle morn, in a time that lies ahead,
we will rise in flight together
amidst the wisp of clouds and the dim of dawn
to follow a sound that calls to both of us,
one that could not reach us in decades past.

From Never to Maybe

You came to me in the summer of unsure,
when never gave way to maybe
and the intense sun appeared to dazzle
rather than to sear.

I was not looking to be rescued
or even to be loved.
I was not looking for anything at all.
Still you came to me with eyes of possibility
and led me from the chaos to the thaw
so I could hope and dream again,
of gypsy moths and gypsy girls
and firelight that tells fortunes in its flames.

I think I will dance like that again
in measured beat and rhythm.
I think I will also sing to the stars
that light my way.
I know I will see your face when I close my eyes,
for that is why you brought me here: to remember.

Poem-Like

There is a poem in everything we do.
It is in the rhythm of our words
that punctuate long conversations.
It is in the cadence of our stride
as we walk the campus track.

It is in the spontaneity
of our laughter that undulates in the dark.
It is in the silence of our hurt
as it strains toward the edge.

There is a poem in everything we do
but I cannot always capture it,
for it shrinks from definition and structure,
much preferring whimsy and song.

Billy Collins' Words

That frigid pre-Christmas night as I read Billy Collins' poetry
while you lay curled up in cold and pain,
I wondered what he would have thought about his words
ricocheting from the blank wall to the sterile cabinets
in the small emergency room.

You fastened upon my voice as I dipped from page to page,
lighting upon this image or that,
as a purposeful bee might zig-zag on a silky spring afternoon.

I read in soft doses, watching your features relax, your eyes close,
and I paused, giving thanks to Billy
for the comfort he provided that could not be measured
or doled out in pretty pastel pills from a small paper cup.

Instead, his words infused that comfortless space
with warmth, curiosity, and humor,
bringing a trace of a smile to your lips,
transporting us to a more benign place.

Poetic Justice

Your eyes are as luminous
as the moon glow that bathes this blistering day,
the softness a salve for all things broken and torn.
In sorrow their azure is deep, dark, fathomless.
In moments of gypsy-whimsy, they acquire the sparkle
of sapphires in the sun.

Your voice is a rhapsody in itself: silky, lilting notes
that sail like a kite in mid-March trying to attain new heights—
or that dip and curve into finger-light caresses,
a slow tango, if you please,
perhaps on a gentle, rainy afternoon.

Your moods, meandering and trickling in no particular fashion,
can flash in bold strokes or steep in calm pastels.
The trick is to savor them both.
There is no existing word that defines you,
this deeply visceral being who has again claimed my heart.

Your Books

I study your bookshelves and smile.
This is not a system fashioned by Dewey Decimal and Marian the
    librarian
where the books are lined straight, corners perfect,
and spines ram-rod erect like soldiers, the rank and file.

Hardly so.

Your scatterings of reading interest are well thumbed,
passages lovingly highlighted or underlined,
corners nonchalantly and unself-consciously bent,
spines relaxed, some in a casual James Dean slouch
with no air of self-importance but with self-esteem intact.

The array of titles speaks volumes about you:
your keen regard for countless thoughts and ideas
translated into decipherable words and fine print,
as well as your reverence for shared solitude
with these friends bound in covers hard and soft.

My Wish

I wish for you a sweet repose
wherever you may be.
I wish to push the clouds from you
and set your lost heart free.

May gentle breezes rock your soul
like a dingy in the bay.
May mountain pines lift spirits high
and cast all gloom away.

You'll never know how well I see
what makes you who you are,
and while deep hurt does leaves its mark,
my core it will not scar.

Totems against Disaster

I give to you a tumi knife,
symbol of Peru—
this one carved and etched in wood,
its lines and curves made smooth by many hands.

Ancients used it for a scalpel, its arrow point sharp and precise;
it also appeared in special rites, a symbol of blessings
for a harvest's generous bounty—
in other words, a multi-purposeful implement.

For you, though, my love,
the tumi has transcended time to take this form.
When worn on its slender cord around your neck
it will become your totem against disaster.
When my arms are absent, it will protect you,
it will orient you when you are steering too far left or right.

I ask for nothing in return.
My totem against disaster is now you.

Glass Jars and Dixie Cups

I sometimes reflect on the fireflies of summer,
their sudden arcs of light in the nighttime sky.
Blink twice and you would miss their brief, erratic glow.

It seemed most dodged the eager reach
of a glass jar in one hand, hole-punched lid in the other.
The not-so-careful few found sudden captivity
until they extinguished altogether,
destined to be in this world an even shorter time.
It was among my earliest understandings
of the temporal nature of life.

Flash forward—years later and much older now—
someone offers love in a Dixie paper cup.
I should be skeptical after my brush with fireflies,
but the cup seems sturdy enough
and the elixir within is intoxicating.

I hold the cup too long, though,
the bottom soon weakening,
the magic seeping, slowly trickling out
until nothing remains.

Had this love been offered in a glass jar,
the chance of survival might have exceeded
that of those hostage fireflies.
Surely love's properties would have seen to that.

What Lies Between Us

Often what lies between us is a soft gray cat with half-closed eyes
and she forms a solid bridge connecting her love for each of us.

Other times it is the Sunday paper, its multiple sections spread lazily
and non-sequentially between the humps of our bodies beneath
        the quilt.

Occasionally it is the remote control which balances precariously
        atop the covers
while one hand or another shifts programming or volume.

Many times it is your hand or mine reaching instinctively across
        the sheets,
fingers engaged and loosely intertwining, nonverbal relay in
        small pulses.

Now, though, what lies between us are words that penetrate rather
        than evaporate,
reminders we are not perfect beings but fragile ones—
still navigating that confluence of present and past.

Losing You

Losing you
would be like having April and May erased from the calendar—
gaping and barren, the keenly felt absence
of the delicate crocus sending its shoots aboveground;
of the sweet flush of a more benign sun;
of the advent of mud puddles that beg for jumping and giggling;
of baseball and soccer fields still soft from morning rain;
of emerging from winter's heavy shadow into the heart of spring.

Losing you
would be unthinkable, for like missing April and May
the world would not be as full of cheer and hope,
and my life would be less with your loss.

Pseudoglyphs

You offered up appeasements
and I took them—
while pretending they had never been presented before—
those subtexts that floated
in the sounds behind your words
sounds that glided smoothly
(if not a bit thickly)
as though you were boating on a lake
drunk on mead.

You offered up enticements
and I wanted them—
giddy gifts such as game shows offer:
large and expensive, small but precious,
and I found myself clasping my hands
my hopeful head bobbing,
all the while decoding the now familiar hieroglyphs
composed of your vocal nuance
and the words springing from them,
recalling the flatness of their affect.

But this time I choose not to participate,
finally tiring of the archaeology of the game.
These patterned offerings are but pseudoglyphs.
symbols of falsehoods,
symbols I recognize and now refuse.

Be Mindful

God speed, my love, and find your way
wherever that may be.
The tides, they change, the swells, they ebb,
the truth is often dark as tea.

The road may cleanse your troubled soul,
your heart may find its string.
Your mind may join the wanderlust
which leaves a hollow ring.

Be mindful what your visions seek,
their paths may tempt you yet.
Don't stray too far from what is near:
the love that you just met.

A Delicate Truce

We maintain a delicate truce,
anchored by a gossamer love stretched taut,
tethered by determination and a commitment to vows.

How we got here hangs heavily between us,
a luminescent question mark that sways uncertainly,
somewhat like a Chinese lantern in the evening breeze.

But here we are,
struggling to comprehend this silky tightrope
both resilient and fragile all at once.

We count on the thread to hold
as we strive for that delicate balance to bridge the chasm
so we can perhaps meet in the middle.

In the Desert Silence of the Night

When the ebony crow flies from his nest
taking leave on his wing without turning back,
then your gut should flutter and bounce.
You will know that I have flown
from that uncertain region of your heart.

There can be no place for me in that desert
where courage fled from fear of having
to test—no, prove—itself,
that place where the soul thirsts
for chance, for change,
and you offer only barren sameness.

As the crow knows that his nest
no longer serves its purpose—
his mate killed the year before,
his offspring finally chased away—
so must I understand my vigil is also empty.

The crow, watchful with his beady eye,
will no doubt soar and find and perhaps forget.
My course will not be as simple,
for everywhere I travel I am certain
to feel your heartbeat.
It will thunder in the desert silence of the night.

Where All Things Begin

Walking toward the east, where the new day begins,
I come to you with open hands.
Look at my treasures:
In this hand I hold my heart, frightened and still
as the doe who listens for the hunter's gun.
In the other hand my soul is a prism, and the light
from your eyes glances off each facet
so that something new is discovered and revealed.

I show these to you as I have to no other
knowing you could snatch my heart, fling it to the wilds,
shattering my soul so that the minuscule pieces
could catch no light again.

I have known men who would do that.

But the wind tells me you are different
and advises me to walk with you,
to take this journey together,
still heading toward the east
where all new things begin.

Half Anniversary

Love notes chime softly
on this rainy half-anniversary,
this mid-November seemingly uncertain
about which way to turn:
Lean back into Indian summer
or brace for the hibernation ahead?

But today we will bask
in the remembrance of a clear day in May
when we pledged self-written vows
and we two joined as one.

Miscellany

Southwest Meditation

Within the pueblo's adobe walls
the drone of the highway is subdued
by humming potters and weavers
and children waving scarves tied to sticks,
running as if launching kites.

A young mother with sleeping infant
wrapped snugly in black shawl
mixes harina with water and deft hands
making her tortillas under the cloudless sky.

An abuelo wise with many years
carves totems for two grandsons—
a coyote for one, bear for the other—
spinning the animals' stories as he was told.

Next to a murmuring fountain
potted cacti arch and stretch toward the sun,
grateful to be one of Nature's houseguests.

The Poem I Was Meant to Write

In the space between my thoughts,
in the silence that came to linger,
an ant crawled across this page at a snail's pace
causing me to stop.

My momentum broken, I halted,
pen in hand, pondering.
Was what I had to write as important
as the mission that had this purposeful ant routing his way
across this lined page to reach some destination?

In the end it didn't really matter.
I had begun staring out the large paned window
and my crafted thought drifted away
like the yellow leaves on the fruitless mulberry
breaking loose and sifting to the ground.

The ant finished crossing the sea of white page,
finding then safe passage on the dark pine paneling
that would lead him where he needed to be.

Perhaps this is the poem I was really meant to write.

The Dairyette Girls
(for Dorothy and Rose)

Those mid-afternoons when we would pack our bags,
laden often with assignments to grade,
those times we gratefully shed our professor personas
and the preoccupations that ordered our days,
on those occasions we three became the Dairyette Girls.

Over burgers and fries, frosty root beer in mugs,
and squeezed in a cramped, red leatherette booth
at a nearby drive-in that had seen much better days,
we would sigh and giggle much as close knit teen girls
must surely have done some sixty years before—
girls with smooth and unlined faces,
shiny hair pulled back in pony tails that bounced—
the pert misses, the original Dairyette Girls.

But those days when we merrily departed campus,
moods buoyed by camaraderie and the prospect of fries,
conversations spanning family and thoughts of retirement
with occasional sprinkles of gossip for dessert,
during those hours we three were the Dairyette Girls,
our laughter as full as the girls' hopes before us
and our age more graceful and resplendent.

A Window and a Ball

What is it about a window that beckons a ball,
almost like crooking a finger
and showing a sultry shoulder?

A ball is helpless to respond,
will change its trajectory to follow the sirens' call,
will hurtle past a boy's upstretched hands,
past another's ears,
alongside a chorus of muffled groans
as its destination becomes clear.

Snared at last,
glass shattering in all directions,
the ball realizes upon contact
that it never really had a chance—
destined as it was for a six-paned window
instead of a baseball glove—
its final resting place an area rug
rather than a patch of St. Augustine.

All because the window played temptress that afternoon
and the ball had no recourse but to answer her call.

The Stories of Elders

The melodies of angels sound no sweeter than the words that spill
from your hearts, your spirits,
from the reservoirs that collect your history—
as precious as spring rainwater stored in casks.

Skaters on a newly frozen pond glide no more gracefully
than the stories that issue from those events, those people,
from those places that bear the imprint of your beings—
as indelible as a child's handprint on a parent's soul.

Continue onward, sweet friends, to the next plateau,
to the next vista, to the next rainbow—
where more stories await, already forming
in your eyes as they span what still lies ahead,
what beckons from the curve of the next bend,
as magnetic as love that is right.

Feline Tendencies

Rumbling purr, kneading paws,
a feline stretch, and this calico
trades pensive for somnolent and,
reaching lazily with her left paw,
takes a half-hearted swipe at the catnip mouse by her side.

I, too, know this feeling
as I gaze at the white flurries
sifting gracefully from the heavy clouds.
I, too, yearn to stretch and curl up in a ball.
I am not a cat,
but I can purr.

La Pantera

In the sunlit-dappled garden
she moves with stealth,
sleek, gray feline form blending with shadows—
green-gray eyes darting with sudden movements.

Her belly flattens,
and with half-closed eyes she serpentines
between the caladiums and the coleus
to arrive behind the stalks of larkspur,
their startling blue spears shielding her frame
until she POUNCES—lightning quick—
on the gecko ascending the fence.
In that moment she is la pantera,
and the noise in her throat is wild and proud.

A Discourse on Cracks

It seems that everything is vulnerable to cracks:
old linoleum and textured walls,
fine china and porcelain fillings.
Even an ordinary sidewalk is a threat to our mother's back.

Cracks also appear in our lives:
hairline splits in our thin veneers,
deep fissures in our relationships,
not to mention the weak foundation
that supports our conscience
(which even our mothers may know nothing about).

An attempt to plaster these telltale spots
is only successful until the next crack appears—
jagged—and spawning arteries
whose branches signal that all does not bode well
for the length of the floor or the wall,
for the sugar bowl or the tooth,
for the surfaces of our feelings,
for the fragile love barely clinging
for the tenuous strain between right and wrong,
for the deep indentations in sidewalks all around
that paralyze children from taking a step.

Only So Many Autumns

There are only so many autumns to embrace—
that delicious filling between slices of summer and winter:
the most delectable part of nature's sandwich.

The first harbinger brings such subtle hint—
a slight shift in dawn's sweet breeze
that makes us want to lift our noses
as a dog might sniff a familiar scent
and find pleasure in the association.

Then comes the shortening of the day,
barely discernible at first—only minutes actually—
but we sense the ticking of nature's internal clock,
much as we become alert to the ticking down of our own.

Which brings us back to the awareness
that we have only so many autumns to claim—
only so many color-laced leaves to kick and scuffle,
only so many crisp afternoons to hug our sweater-clad selves tighter
as we hear the voice of childhood calling it a day.

Early Morning Yoga

On my mat in the quiet of dawn
I am alone in the midst of others,
using silence and a dim room
to frame my thoughts,
to set my intention,
to listen to my breath.

My body responds slowly at first,
still missing the warmth of soft sheets and the cover of sleep.
Soon, though, it carries me through the poses,
faltering a bit in warrior three—
as balancing on one leg does not come naturally at six a.m.—
grasping for stability in half moon as fingertips
graze the floor, leg extends back,
arm and head raise upward . . .
searching for balance yet again.

Then on to a series of graceful flows, fluid and energetic,
creating heat and strength.
I am grateful when my body can sink into half pigeon,
hips protesting only mildly in the deep stretch
before transitioning to an inversion
and unfolding gently into savasana:
final
resting
pose.

Namaste.

Ahimsa

In yoga we practice with ahimsa,
discipline without violence.
It is an intention we set when rolling out our mats,
not bringing unnecessary harm to our bodies
during this dedicated time of mindful practice.
Our purpose is to nurture, not to violate.

Off our mats
in this unsettling and conflicted world,
we should exercise patience;
we should exercise respect;
we should be grateful for every kindness extended us.
If we practice with ahimsa,
then we may live life with ease.

Forgiveness Is a Salve

Anger hollows the spirit's core
eviscerating it from the inside out,
leaving it raw and barren,
more barren than a wasteland.

You must protect your soul, my friend,
from desolation that burns by day,
from collapse into cold so utterly stark
it blinds you from the truth at hand.

Forgiveness is a salve, sweet one,
that medicates the constant ache,
dissolves corrosion of self-doubt,
and ushers in the breath of light.

Sacrifice to the River-God

At twenty-three
I lost my first student to suicide.
During holiday break,
while home in Iowa, he became a sacrifice to the river-god.
I try to picture a lone figure on the banks
perhaps with arms raised upward,
eyes closed, waiting for a sign.
Then looking down at the icy froth
where the current showed life signs of its own,
he saw better still, a release.

I read with pangs of conscience
the campus report of his death,
the words "break-up with a girl"
swimming before my eyes,
and I saw him at once—
and as I still do—
a mop of dark hair,
a face intensely expressive
and framed in dark glasses.
I see more clearly
the scribbled journal entries assigned,
and the syllables of despair
as he repeated time after time
that he was unlucky in love.

I hope,
though I can't remember,
but I would like to think
that I jotted a phrase of encouragement,
that I did not totally discount
his anguish and distress
as I read through his private thoughts.
But if I did,
he may have read it as a platitude—
a token response to a lovelorn student.

It would seem
his cry for mercy
was more easily assuaged by the river-god
who promised him no more pain
as he swallowed this young man whole.

This Warm, Starry Night

In the middle of the shimmer
of this warm, starry night,
young and seasoned lovers gaze in pure delight
at the rapture of the moon beams that dance sprightly in the light,
in the light of the warm, starry night.

In the pale light of the glimmer
on this warm, starry night,
the burdened seek their answers from this luminescent sight;
the beggars and the thieves regard the moon glow as a blight
and curse the light of this warm, starry night.

In the dewy, waning shimmer
of this warm, starry night,
the fingerlings of moon rays reach down from their height
and sweep away the shadows to form an entrance for the light,
bringing closure to the warm, starry night.

Train Ride

This line between stayin' and goin'
and livin' and dyin'
is a real blur now.

Like bein' on a train in that observin' car.
Lookin' out the window and watchin' the sweep
of land and hills and sometimes water,
watchin' all become one for the instant they pass your eyes.

My, it gets dizzy, and what with the rumblin'
of the engines and the jerkin' along the track,
it's all a body can do to stay intact.

I took a train a long time ago.
That's how I know what it's like.
I rode it from Ohio to Texas,
left my family to marry a rancher and never went back.
Nineteen then and full of piss and vinegar,
my daddy liked to say.
Never liked the hard times, but never shied
away from them neither.
I recall bein' a tad nervous takin' a train
to meet the swirlin' dust and sand of West Texas.
Sure wasn't what I was used to,
but love makes everythin' look better.

That blasted sand, though, took the design
right out of my heirloom rug from home,
like it was bent on erasin' my past.
That delicate fleur de lis soon faded
and became a dusty blur.
Like this line between stayin' and goin',
between livin' and dyin'.

I'm near ready for this train ride to end.
I'm ready to go home.

Another Rug Story

I know two rug stories that speak to loss,
both tragic for different reasons.
One I have already written of—
about an heirloom treasure that traveled
from Ohio to Texas.
I happened upon this second account
in an oral tale that has haunted me
for some time now.
It goes like this:

An old timer tells of a Nebraska prairie woman
who one morning took down to a string of trees
her young daughter and a rug.
The young child ran about in the shade and cool breeze
while her mother draped and secured the braided rug
over a low sturdy limb,
proceeding to beat many months of dirt and dust
with the largest rock she could find.

Black-billed magpies yakked overhead, a strong sun looked down
as she worked the rug until tiring.
Her daughter no longer in sight, the mother called and called,
finally throwing the rock down to search.

A few yards out she stopped cold,
chest tightening, face paling.
Turning back, she walked heavily to the rug
still tightly fastened to the limb with pieces of rope.

Making her way to the other end,
the part of the rug she had not yet hoisted and cleaned,
the woman screamed, drowning out the magpies.
For wrapped inside, as if in a tight cocoon,
her small child lay curled, silent and still,
life beaten out of her.

The young prairie mother never considered loss as an option.
Two days later she hanged herself from the same tree

where her daughter had last played and lived.
Two neighbor men took down the bloodstained rug,
their wives tending to the broken husband and father.
Two graves were dug, two female spirits reunited.
The old timer's point: Life was just plain hard then,
which is why this rug story should also be told.
Now you know this story, too.

Middles

I like middles.
They are familiar, comfortably predictable.
They bear substance and bring quiet ease to sameness.

Beginnings float on bubbles of hope.
In their newness, they portend wishful optimism.
The heart steps out first, followed then by the head.

Endings are grainy and finite.
They have no patience with vacillation,
no trust in second guesses.
The outcome is whatever it comes out to be.

I much prefer middles
and will choose the cream filling
of an Oreo cookie
every single time.

Etchings

We leave our marks everywhere:
Childhood visions etched into brick;
Heights recorded on a doorframe or wall;
Hearts earnestly carved into rough bark of trees;
Chalk designs colored onto neighborhood sidewalks;
Tattoo ink pierced into canvas of skin;
Sentiments engraved onto metal.

And not to forget—
all the multifold touches of tender thought
etched deeply into the human heart.

When Clay Treasures Travel

Surrounded
by clay and silver and turquoise
she sits in silence on the square:
a wizened brown-skinned figure
whose leather-lined face and hands
tell many stories about her life and craft.

She watches curiously
as tourists pass before her
murmuring praise for her careful work:
the delicate yet robust pots
smoothed to perfection
by well-taught hands;
simple gleaming silver pieces,
elaborate inlaid turquoise wonders—
all these a part of her,
each a fragment of her experience.

The Acoma woman
makes a transaction,
listens to the delight of the buyer,
nods in understanding,
for *her* delight still enshrouds
the clay object—
a bonus for the buyer.

That is the way it is,
she wants to say.
When you buy from me
you enter my circle,
you become part of the connection.

She takes leave at the end
of the clay treasure
that has changed hands.
In low whisper
she invokes the spirit of her People
to follow that part of her soul

that lies wrapped in newspaper,
destined for Maine,
far from the dancing grounds of the sun.

Literary Pigeons

Pigeons wobbling on the other side of the classroom window
squabble at times like a couple who knows one another too well—
or not well enough.
Face to face, squat and sturdy,
they peck and flutter—
beaks opening ominously, eyes beady and intense.

Occasionally, almost on cue,
they will pause and stare into the window
as if the words *Ibsen* and *irony*
hold a place in their collective memory
and they sense they must listen.

Their attention span is all too brief, however,
for soon the pair leaves the ledge in a spurt of gray and blue,
flying to the opposite roof
where the squabbling begins anew.

Tableau

Imagine passing a neighborhood sidewalk
perhaps expecting to find a girl's game of hopscotch
carefully drawn in deep violet chalk,
but seeing instead a simple tableau:
mother and child—
motionless, soundless, hand reaching for hand,
the action almost consummated and unshackled by time and space.
The mother's eyes are luminous with joy,
the child's gaze fixed and trusting,
all under a cloudless June sky.

Consider the desire to step just inside
those deliberately colored borders,
curious to join the two fleeing figures
so delicately and innocently captured for eternity—
that is, until the next rainstorm sweeps through
leaving a soft violet puddle in its wake.

The Measure of a Hand

What is the full measure of a hand—
four slender fingers and opposable thumb by their side?

A hand in an x-ray can lay bare its bones
naked, unembarrassed by its skeletal form.

It can softly lay smooth a lace heirloom cloth
with long recalled care and social grace.

It can trace in a mirror the outline of its mate,
bringing a delicate though ephemeral union.

It can graze a cheek either in anger or love,
leaving a raised welt or the blush of caress.

It can deliberately dance along black and white keys,
tinkling a trail of melodic notes.

And a hand can pen sad farewell in loops and curves
when all other attempts have failed.

What is the full measure of a hand—
four slender fingers and opposable thumb by their side?

Perhaps it is all of the above—and more.

Epistle to a Fallen American

I need to tell you:
It is an honor to care for your body,
to gently remove the crusted blood
from your rough-edged nails
and your freckled, sunburned arms.

I need to tell you:
It is a privilege to clean and shine
the saint's medal that lay against your neck
and polish your boots so that no scuffs remain.
I do so gently and with great pride.

I need to tell you:
It is with deference that I select a clean shirt
to replace the one torn and singed
and not wholly intact,
and to smooth the wrinkles from the new fabric.

I must tell you:
My hand trembles as I fold *your* hands,
as I step back to pay homage to your youth,
to your bravery, to the meaning of your life.

I salute you.

On a Flawless Summer Morning

The woman in azure silk,
not given a choice to stay
where she had lived her whole life,
chose to die—
tumbling from a Huey chopper
while her surroundings still felt familiar—
tumbling almost gently into a rice paddy
of soft liquid brown.

The pilot watched bewildered,
nimble as the woman was, quick to leave her seat;
the other refugees took up wailing.
She had been one of them until that moment of decision.

The woman in ruined silk
remained unmoving in the lush bed of rice
with a pale straw bag still clutched to her heart.
Saigon had dictated relocations,
but the woman who did not want to leave her home
chose otherwise
on that flawless summer morning.

A Different Kind of Anniversary

It was a Monday,
a quite ordinary day in June—
innocuous as all uneventful beginnings of weeks—
until late afternoon when the heat of the day
was its most intense and the wind brought no relief.

An ordinary day, which became alarmingly extraordinary
when the meter box exploded
showering the patio with shards of shrapnel,
the fuse box on the other side
sending corresponding sparks that ignited—
then engulfed—and then spread smoke and flames
throughout the ductwork.

And all the while I watched and waited
for help to arrive in the form of four large fire trucks
with men and hoses and axes.

I waited on the front lawn
while two cats remained trapped inside
and I felt heartsick, helpless, and defeated.

I watched as a home became a structure
stripped of its expression and identity,
finding in that transformation
a horrific and surreal awareness
as I pondered what the days ahead would be like.

I waited, suspended, in the smoky twilight
for two sturdy helmeted saviors to emerge,
each carrying a cat under an arm—
two terrified felines soot-singed but still alive.

And so it is I mark this anniversary—
this one being the seventh of that fiery blaze—
with gratitude.

From the ashes on that day in June
a damaged structure became again a house
which then comfortably eased into a home
from which memories—both good and bad—
were erased and a rebirth was allowed.
After some time I arose from those ashes, too,
finding a new self stronger than my old self,
becoming both humbled and renewed.

Salvation by Fire

We are never more helpless than when we are burning,
pooling into ourselves—
raw feelings melting—
the goo seeping out the raw-boned edges
and forming puddles of all that had been.

Regeneration comes slowly, fitfully,
the pace in accordance with our capacity
to surrender the past
(O why won't people let go?)
and the willingness to explore what lies over the hill
and within our new heart . . .
where seedlings sprout in the aftermath.

No Two Moments the Same

Hallowed is this place where the hollowed core resides.
Impervious to nothing, it is open to everything,
yet it fears not.
It understands that time is fluid,
no two moments the same,
and thus it remains amorphous to accommodate all change.

Universal is this place that knows the tumble of joy and loss
with often only a split second between,
yet it grieves not.
It understands that time is fluid,
no two moments the same,
and thus concedes that nothing can last forever.

Out of Something Ordinary

You know how it goes—
in a gathering of friends and folks
the question arises:
Where were *you*
when JFK was assassinated?
when the planes crashed into the Twin Towers?
during that tragic Boston Marathon bombing?
Responses flow in crystalline form,
detailed, vivid, etched forever,
the extraordinary events
rising from otherwise ordinary days.

I cannot recall where I was yesterday at noon
or when I last smelled the fragrant wisteria
because nothing momentous
ascended from the ashes of those times.

But today, during the simple process
of sewing a button on a turquoise dress,
I felt that life would never be the same.
I cursed the button for the lump forming,
settling in my throat.
I suddenly realized I understand less about human nature
than ever before
because I have been completely wrong about you.

This staggering awareness came to me
while engaged in mind-numbing activity,
in the simple repetition of needle and thread.

A revelation out of something ordinary.

A Pillow Note

It may be the pork chop wrapped in foil and left in the oven
will be too stringy or tough.
At 7:00 when you called to say you were headed home,
it was still succulent and warm,
seasoned the way that used to bring a smile
and a compliment for the cook.

You may wish to pass on the whipped potatoes
which, at 7:00, were still lightly mounded on the plate,
the flecks of garlic, pepper, and butter
lending an appetizing appeal.
Now they are no doubt cold and stiff,
a culinary corpse of sorts.

And had you arrived home at 7:15 as you indicated you would,
your senses would have been treated
to that delectable yeast aroma
that only homemade rolls can yield.
Alas—I fear they mostly resemble musket balls now—
lonely arsenal on the cookie sheet.

Sorry I missed your call at 8:30 announcing your reason for delay.
I was putting the twins down, finally,
though they wanted so desperately to see you.
But I kissed them twice: once for me and once for you,
figuring you would want it that way.

Perhaps you stopped for a burger on the way home, late as it was.
If so, may you not be visited by late night reflux,
that dastardly visitor.

Despite best laid plans going awry,
Happy Birthday anyway.

Pancake Panacea

In the aftermath of numbing hurt,
a hurt no woman should expect, much less endure—
not at twenty-one, not at any age—
I found myself waiting out the dawn,
waiting for the signal of the mourning doves.

At their sound I tiptoed from my room,
stepped outside to frigid air and a weak Texas sun,
headed gingerly down the stairway,
walked by the pool ignored during winter,
approached the doorway of a friend and knocked.

Pete, gentle and gifted musician from Rhode Island,
sleepy Pete answered while shielding his eyes and peering
into the milky bright morning light.
He stared, stunned, noting my bruised face,
my neck punctuated with sharp cuts.

Helpless to know what to do—much less say—
Pete held and listened, rocked and comforted
and finally did what he always did
when he did not know what else to do:
Pete made pancakes.

As we ate them in silence, the honeyed syrup
commingling with the salt of new tears,
I thanked Pete softly for his friendship,
for the healing power of his pancakes
when nothing else made sense,
when the safety of his kitchen did.

Asking for Grace

At the end of the day
as noise subsides, fatigue recedes,
I ask simply for grace to soften the edges
of truth and despair.
I reach for memories both gentle and dear,
wanting them here, finding them there.

I watched as my father struggled for words,
a man once stalwart and wise.
I saw my sweet mother solemnly gaze
at her world grown more narrow in size.
I wished to enclose them with arms calm and strong,
but at the close of such days
I asked only for grace to soften the edges
of truth and despair.
I reached for memories both gentle and dear,
wanting them here as they eluded me there.

Then and Now

No more the heart replete with hope,
no more the moment's whim take hold.
The time to dare to wish was then,
the time to touch the ground is now.

Dreams are fancy, with eyes bright and wide,
truth is forceful, removing all blinds.
Magic in love shows its own sleight of hand,
illusion entrances 'til the next trick unfolds.

Gather what's fragile of all that remains,
find a safe place to bury or hide.
Protect your own heart from love's silver tongue.
Find peace in experience, most golden of all.

Dissonance

Yesterday the earth quaked in California,
causing fear and chaos, leaving tremors in its wake.

This afternoon the aspens were quaking in New Mexico,
fluttering and whispering while their white trunks
remained anchored in the ground, solid and secure
in the stillness which precedes a mountain rainstorm
and leaves a freshness in its wake.

And though it is clear which phenomenon we prefer,
we accept this balancing act that nature must perform—
disruption versus serenity—
our own balancing acts no doubt equally dissonant.

No Such Thing

"There is no such thing as too much love."
Such is Madam Juda's pronouncement
as she sits amid her crystals
and surveys her multi-ringed hands.
Her laugh is a languid breeze
that teases my protestations,
lifting them and then letting them land
with a thud.

"Too much love?"
she echoes disdainfully.
"It shouldn't take a clairvoyant to tell you
what a fool you are.
Where once you were starved,
now you are replete—
and you would question it?"
Now her laughter tinkles like the charms
that dangle from her heavy silver bracelet,
like chimes glancing off crystal prisms
in the light.

"No such thing," Madam Juda repeats,
sighing to her napping cat.
"There's just no such thing as too much love."

The Remainder Shop

If you find yourself searching for the elusive,
why not pay a visit to the Remainder Shop?
Not merely remnants or leftovers,
this shop holds so much more.
It is the repository for all things no longer needed,
perhaps no longer wanted.
It relies on happenstance and misfortune,
on whimsy and afterthought.

Wander the aisles noting the curiosities:
A slender ring whose tale no one will know;
A faded photograph much handled and worn;
A new beaded dress bought in hope but released;
A book treated poorly that no longer matters;
A record's one scratch that ruins the whole;
A lone doeskin glove still mourning its mate;
A ship on its side marooned forever.

And then on a day quite ordinary,
on a day of no expectation
other than idle curiosity
of what remainders might lie within,
on a day when serendipity pleads to be unleashed,
perhaps we will come upon each other.
If you get there first, please wait for me.
We will look beyond what is broken and lost,
discovering what is still salvageable within us
and, together, become that rare find.

One Summer in San Francisco

During a cold season one summer in San Francisco
I happened upon a parrot
muttering the Ten Commandments
while perched in front of the town hall.
People waved napkins wildly in the air,
unions stood uneasily at the side,
and the parrot concluded by adamantly squawking
that he preferred Cracker Jacks to applause.

My sister was home calculating and ruminating
over the x-factor of some strange symbol.
My mother was searching Google for a long-lost love.
And I? I was listening to a parrot quoting biblical verse.

Maybe I was catching the flu.

Winter's Hues

This winter's night the world is black and blue,
moon's slight sliver showing through
to reveal the bruising left by day—
the aftermath of lashing winds and bitter cold
and a landscape aching and worn.

With dawn's delicate presence
a sprinkling of silver fairy frost
will soften midnight's harsh bleakness,
will provide a tender salve to raw edges,
will deliver a balm for the battered spirit.

Hungers

In the utter stillness of pre-dawn quiet,
the mind lingers on hungers that cannot return,
recalling the brine and the sweet.
Memory arises, always a curious reminder,
filtering nothing to keep us honest and true.
The hungers of then sport rose-colored nothings
blurred as they are in memory's strong hold.
The hungers of now crave edge over precedence
hoping to quell any traces still tinged
with longing and reminiscent glow.

So we move on both forward and backward
tumbling with hungers that know not their place,
bombarding our senses with recall, with insistence
when the will is half-slumbering,
when time hovers lightly between night and morn,
when our being rumbles for more.

Raven Mocker

Yesterday an apparition stood before me,
backdrop to an early dawn,
his wizened shape fading in, then fading out
as the day took hold.
Ancient, unguarded eyes enveloped me,
a somnolent embrace that rocked me from my dreams,
and a whisper slid over me, gliding like a snake:
"I am Raven Mocker."

Most feared of all Cherokee witches,
he crossed to me with the alacrity of youth
and his withered hand reached for my heart.
His shape became as amorphous as the chant
that undulated in my ears,
sounds that gripped my chest
as he pulled my heaving heart from well within.

Then intoned in my language, voice resonant and clear:
"I take your sadness and sew it into my own skin.
Like patchwork, I piece it to my own.
O Little One, return to life
for it is not yet your turn, not yet your time," he rasped.
"I am cursed to make you well."

My heart fluttered in the air, a hummingbird of sorts
in search of nectar to sustain body and soul.
It flitted to the gaping hole and quieted.
Then I fully awoke, alone yet light,
and from the doorway Raven Mocker
tugged at his skin, stretching it this way and that,
and moved on his way.

Between

Between the realm of somewhere and the significance of goodbye,
rivers swell proudly, mountains breathe quietly,
and soldiers are bound to die.

Between the realm of somewhere and the significance of goodbye,
petals lift softly, poems unfold gently,
and lovers consent to lie.

Between the realm of somewhere and the significance of goodbye,
hummingbirds flit lightly, leaves descend lazily,
and the lonely release a sigh.

Between that realm of somewhere and the significance of goodbye,
canyons still echo, sapphires still sparkle,
and most of us continue to try.

At the End

When I become a silver elder,
hands gnarled but eyes still bright,
I will sprinkle the ground before me
with all the blessings I have stored within:
One corner
for the childhood nurturers
whose guidance kept me steady;
another corner
for the lovers and friends
whose belief kept me strong;
still another
for my stalwart sons
whose trust kept me stable;
the fourth
for the lifework that kept me content.

Those anchors acknowledged,
I will survey the center
spreading the remainder of the precious seeds
to honor still another:
You, who offered the torch of passion and dreams,
the gift of second chance.
Then I will step back,
silver but grounded,
awaiting eventual rest.

Haiku Collection

Like Footprints on the Moon

Your imprint on me—
like those footprints on the moon—
is indelible.

After all this time—
the tread unmistakable—
my heart still stands still.

I yearn for footfalls
belonging only to you,
yet silence answers.

26 Untitled Haiku

Amsterdam sunrise—
hint of pink beneath the fog—
prelude to the day.

Ah banana moon,
the curve of your back is soft
in the black sky.

Ash clouds streak the dawn,
but wait—pink blush arises.
Sky cheeks are glowing.

Aerial ballet:
Hummingbirds poised in mid-air
flutter gracefully.

Dark clouds usher dawn,
fingerlings stretching, yawning.
Yoga beckons now.

Ink blots in the sky,
pale blue liquid peering through.
Morning has broken.

Maple leaves shimmer
as early Spring evening light
creates crimson glow.

Patches of pale light,
like ice floes in a dark sea,
dot the dawning sky.

Slender crescent moon,
sliver in indigo sky,
bids adieu to the night.

Snow pierces twilight,
rustles like silken curtain
across the lone road.

Yellow daffodils
bow to late winter snowfall,
listening for Spring.

Haloed winter moon,
soft against the starry night,
bless us with your grace.

Sky of inky black,
cover me, cloak me tightly.
Let me dream wisely.

So, still waning moon,
teller of fortunes and fate:
What is to be mine?

Sweeping purple sage,
like heather on the moorlands,
graces the school yard.

Take heart, tender soul,
and stand on tip-toes to reach:
magic awaits you.

Through the gauzy scrim
pastel colors peep and yawn
announcing the dawn.

Wind, relentless wind—
brash wind insults, spitting sand,
seeking a target.

Winter's cold breath
leaves light frosting on rooftops,
clean edged and pristine.

Shooting star above,
serene pasture land below:
Change is on the cusp.

Fingers dance on keys
pausing now and then to rest.
The mind is elsewhere.

Feline stretches paw,
reaching for flying insect.
The catch is complete.

Silhouetted trees
sway softly in early light,
like women dancing.

Moon slips behind clouds
then emerges all golden—
a quick disrobing.

Against a stiff sea
a seagull perches, stoic
in the wind and mist.

A full moon rising:
bright orb of abundant light—
a sentry of sorts.

Irish Haiku

These Dublin women
sport their beauty distinctly
clad in patterned skirts.

The Irish drizzle
shadowed us to the train stop.
Farewell, sweet Galway.

Sheep graze in pasture
amidst the heather and gorse.
It is all they know.

The train to Dublin
 rolls past the River Shannon,
current swift and green.

Fog sweeps gracefully
across the Bay of Dingle:
Such a grand beauty.

Another Revelation

A kitten appeared
beneath my deck, abandoned.
I did not keep him.

I almost kept him—
he trusted me already—
but I gave him up.

It is my nature
to rescue and protect
those who come to me.

But now I realize
that I can't always rescue
every lost creature.

Cinquain Collection

8 untitled cinquains

How high
the spirit soars—
lifting from the abyss,
floating among currents and clouds
once more.

Feline
purrs, twitchy dreams
remind me I'm only
human and cannot spare the time
to sleep.

From whence
this love spurts, swells,
and spreads its soundless joy
I do not try to analyze.
I feel.

I rise
to that calm place,
then gather the prana
from the life forces around me.
Come, too.

Really?
In Irish pubs
the men's loo on first floor,
and the women's on the second?
Really?

Thank you
for being there
when no one else would do.
I should have known you would appear.
Again.

Today
in the dim room,
my mat alongside yours,
we flow through poses and deep breaths.
For now.

Siblings
in the hot sun—
two brothers and sister—
give thanks, pay tribute to parents
at graves.

Pantoum Collection

In Spite of the Shadows

In spite of the shadows that cloak this day,
the smile in your eyes casts an ambient glow.
Even in darkness light holds sway,
for hope is what the hopeful sow.

The smile in your eyes casts an ambient glow,
protecting what lies beyond this nebulous turn—
for hope is what the hopeful sow
even when dreams die in fire's lasting burn.

Protecting what lies beyond this nebulous turn,
you ponder your chances, consider your fate.
Even when dreams die in fire's lasting burn,
you decide to plunge forward and not hesitate.

You ponder your chances, consider your fate,
debate whether to follow your head or your heart;
you decide to plunge forward and not hesitate,
more certain than ever of future's fresh start.

Debate whether to follow your head or your heart—
even in darkness light holds sway;
more certain than ever of future's fresh start,
in spite of the shadows that cloak this day.

That Final Time

Until I kissed you that final time
my lips touching lightly upon your moist skin,
I must have forgotten the rhythm and rhyme
in the decoupaged places where I once had been.

My lips touching lightly upon your moist skin
releasing stark tales that became my whole life
in the decoupaged places where I once had been,
lying in slivers as if sliced by a knife.

Releasing stark tales that became my whole life—
a balance of triumphs and varied regrets—
lying in slivers as if sliced by a knife
I took too few chances, hedged too many bets.

A balance of triumphs and varied regrets
nail me to life as if on a cross.
I took too few chances, hedged too many bets;
I spent far too much time focused insanely on loss.

Nail me to life as if on a cross—
I must have forgotten the rhythm and rhyme.
I spent far too much time focused insanely on loss
until I kissed you that final time.

Leaving Not Forever, Just for Now

You ask me where I'm going, your voice so flat and low,
and I tell you once again I feel that I must go.
I'm leaving not forever, just for now.
Those simple words are all I can allow.

I tell you once again I feel that I must go.
Your shoulders hunch, your sighs are soft and slow.
Those simple words are all I can allow.
I'm looking for salvation, not a furrowed brow.

Your shoulders hunch, your sighs are soft and slow.
We let the silence be the only sound.
I'm looking for salvation, not a furrowed brow;
I'm aching for a peace I have not found.

We let the silence be the only sound
and watch as if it's going to take a bow.
Aching for a peace I have not found,
I'm leaving not forever, just for now.

Birthday Pantoum for Adam
(On the Occasion of Your 27th)

The first time your eyes locked into mine,
you gazed steadily, hazel into brown,
surveying the whole of me in one sweeping line:
intent on sight, seemingly oblivious to sound.

You gazed steadily, hazel into brown,
piercing post-glow reverie in one silent look—
intent on sight, seemingly oblivious to sound,
unveiling me, like pages in a book.

Piercing post-glow reverie in one silent look,
signaling you knew me long before,
unveiling me—like pages in a book—
you introduced new content and made me more.

Signaling you knew me long before,
I was at once comforted and sure;
you introduced new content and made me more
and swept me into your instant allure.

Forever swept into your allure
the first time your eyes locked into mine.

Sonnet Collection

A Sonnet for My Father

As night decides it's time to close each day,
so must you now accept the arm of death
and cross the threshold where you now will stay:
a realm that knows not illness, thought, or breath.

So you, my father, trying thus to steer
amidst awareness in a world turned dim,
relinquish hold on what you long deemed dear
and leave this life that's narrowed and grown slim.

Though those who love you grieve you on your way
and mourn the void that you have left behind,
we will take heart that pain no more holds sway
nor does confusion overwhelm your mind.

Your legacy continues to prevail,
and honor lives in what we have to tell.

A Sonnet for My Mother

Your face upturned so slightly in the frame:
dark hair, dark eyes that hold a dreamy look.
Immortalized in time you stay the same
as all the photos in our family book.

So hopeful is the smile that lights your face.
To Texas from Connecticut you came
to carve your future in this foreign place.
You placed your trust, you felt this was no game.

A whirlwind courtship left you wanting more;
you countered parents' wishes, leaving home.
Naïve, perhaps, courageous to the core—
a train ride to the land where cowboys roam.

You lived in Texas longer than the East,
your love for Dad still strong until you ceased.

A Sonnet Lamenting War

The bells rang hollow in the misty night
and clamored in the stillness until dawn;
the battlefield lay foul, a gruesome sight,
and not a single soldier saw the sun.

The mothers and the wives swept 'cross the fields,
the search continued for the one they loved;
their skirts were drenched in dew, their hands were shields,
to block the stench of death that seeped ungloved.

Soft moans escaped the quiet hush of night,
though hardly uttered by the fallen brave.
Instead, the women formed a line of might
and wailed that they could not just one life save.

Before a waning moon and heartsick sun,
the mangled arms and legs all 'round did lie.
the battle carnage stretched forever done;
tears and sobs both rivaled landscape's sigh.

The women's grief was heard throughout the land.
And at its core, the senseless death of man.

Sonnet for a Pilgrim Soul

You hold the key to all that makes me free;
your able hands so practiced and so sure
remove deceit so I may stand and see
that tarnished love, when polished, can shine pure.

You enter from the half-light of my dreams
as if to guide me to a certain door.
I know that nothing's rarely what it seems,
I know that ships don't always reach the shore.

Though fearful I may be, I'm tempted more
to trust that Fate would not mislead again.
So many signs I'm trying to ignore
all point to where my heart has never been.

They key you hold is rusted yet intact.
The door you open brings the pilgrim back.

Sonnet for Hope

When all our dreams are swallowed up by night
and mid-day suns obscured by misery;
when happiness seems captured by a blight
and boats are scattered by an angry sea;

when fragile hope hangs by a dainty thread
and courage falters slightly on the ledge;
when stomachs crave the sustenance of bread
and broken gamblers have no bets to hedge;

when lies bounce off the souls of humankind
and tears no longer soothe the festered sore;
when hearts can't liberate but only bind
and promise quenches children's trust no more;

So the dove appears once more to save.
We learned and suffered more than what we gave.

A Last Sonnet

I see your face in everything I do,
I hear your voice in every word I write,
I miss the fact I cannot be with you,
I wish you had not given up the fight.

You never overcame your fear to trust
and nothing that I did was quite enough.
I watched your courage crumble in the dust,
I waited far too long to call your bluff.

How sad to spurn love's offer at the end,
take leave and stay resolved to not return.
I only tried to show how lives could blend
and rise triumphant from past love's slow burn.

Though certain that our paths were meant to cross,
my heart aches now from such a senseless loss.

Sonnet on Love Eclipsed

I do not understand the how or why,
nor can I comprehend how you must feel;
I only know the well is running dry
and this magnolia's losing all her steel.

The day still sets and rises just the same
and people go about their busy lives.
The question isn't which of us to blame
when both our worlds are now reduced in size.

I struggled to uphold my pledge to you
those sixteen years ago when love was high,
but I can't heal both hearts now torn in two
and neither one of us respects a lie.

To solitude you take a deep, wide bow
and trade your past for some uncertain now.

A Southern Cry

The night they tore old Mississippi down
like lions stripping martyred Christians' flesh,
the genteel folk did try their best to frown,
desirous that these clashing realms not mesh.

These men whose hatred frothed in rabid foam
pursued the hunt unequal from the start;
they heard a call that threatened what they owned,
this cry for justice pierced their southern heart.

Their choice of violence marked ignoble souls,
for how can wrong be noble in God's eyes?
A misplaced anger racking such harsh tolls,
this effort aimed at signaling demise.

But courage trumps man's hatred in the end,
and right will triumph o'er another's sin.

When Love Is Not Enough

When love is not enough to heal life's wounds,
forgive such hurts still seeping from the past,
perhaps it's time to face the truth that looms
and reconcile that what we have won't last.

Despite the tender mercies we've displayed
and all the well-intentioned words we've shared,
dark demons still undo what steps we've made
and all the secrets we have bravely bared.

It's not enough to mingle heartfelt tears,
admire the strengths and attributes we love.
Too soon the awkward moments feel like years;
too soon the clouds obscure the sun above.

Take my hand and squeeze it one last time.
Perhaps you'll find your rhythm, I my rhyme.

Waiting with the Seabird

The day hangs gray and solemn like a vow
and does not heed the sun's desire for light.
Dark claims his right to take control of now
and drapes mid-morning in a sheath of night.

I stand atop a craggy cliff to wait
while boiling whitecaps churn the sea below.
A lonely seabird circles for his mate,
my own lament commingling with his woe.

The day you chose to sail, the sun turned cold
but that did not deter your will one whit.
With purpose strong, your heart and spirit bold,
your course was racked by storm and tempest hit.

I still await your body to be found.
I listen for your name in ocean's sound.

Waltzing Toward Winter

Dedicated to My Memoir Writing Class
at Buckner Retirement Village

You are the red and gold of season's change,
your foliage like a badge you flaunt with pride;
your grand performance heightens nature's range,
your age you do not feel a need to hide.

You waken in the crisp of morning sun;
in sparkling effervescence, mark the day.
A landscape barren, sere, and almost done
assumes your luster, wishes you could stay.

Amid the blust'ry gusts you stand your post,
adorning trees that usually would be bare.
In time the trees will stand alone as ghosts
and miss your vibrant colors and your care.

And when that time arrives, because it must,
before you nod and take a final bow,
look past the season's hues to snow's first crust
and know the time for "then" has come to "now."

So tumble, float, and swirl in downward turns,
and waltz toward winter while the colors burn.

Sonnet on Change

I plan my days in measured lengths of time.
Defining weeks and months mean less to me
as rhythm now means less to me than rhyme.
My inclination now is just to be.

I practice yoga so my soul can thrive
since structure's not the order of my day.
But still I must create to stay alive;
I must produce for that is still my way.

Restrictions lifted, "musts' become my "mays,"
but aiming for key balance keeps me straight.
I treasure small rewards in simple ways
while understanding, too, that some must wait.

Retirement's proved a blessing, not a curse.
The trick is plan for better, not for worse.

Sonnet of Reflection

Remember this about me when I'm gone:
that love did nourish more than any food,
that tender smiles uplifted more than song,
that heartfelt hugs dispelled a somber mood.

And when love beckoned me to come along,
I followed with my heart so full of hope.
I had my children, loved when love was strong;
I met Despair who taught me how to cope.

And of my teaching there is much to tell:
a blend of voices echo from the past,
their stories rise and fall in one great swell—
shared learning that inspired up to the last.

Remember that I leave but for a while.
I'll look for you and know you by your smile.

Tributes

Aunt Edie
(1917-1998)

We leave for you a sign of leafy life
to grace the site where you've been laid to rest
and ease you into soft and dreamless sleep
which marks the end of earthly time.

The slender curve of branch and leaf
will shelter you from brazen northern winds
and drape your bed, as seasons change,
with first dark greens, then lovely scarlet hues.

Echoing songs will resonate
from branches parted in the breeze
and fill your sleep with pleasant sounds,
sweet lullabies of a different kind.

Thus we celebrate your long-lived life
in planting a maple by your side
to remind us of full life now passed
and a bloodline that binds all to one.

John Wadhams
(1954-2014)

No more the dawnings of violet and gray,
No more the harbingers' burst into song.
My wish for you on this soft summer night
is for you to walk gently in the pale white of light.

Oliver: Noble Flame Point Siamese
(1995-2010)

I look for your face behind the door,
for the question mark in your tail,
for any sign of your presence—
something to hint at your return.

Even when I held you that last time,
your body more compliant than usual;
even though I knew I would never look again
into your startling blue eyes,
I willed myself to believe I would still come home
to find you sunning in your favorite spot,
in your favorite reclining pose.

Take flight with the birds you loved to chase,
drift with the cumulus clouds.
You long ago took root in my heart—
now move toward the long sleep in peace.

Prada: Ginger Tabby Extraordinaire
(2004-2017)

You held fast to your brand of catness even to the end,
meandering, though slowly, alongside
the uneven border rocks which lined the garden beds
you so liked to explore.

Your flanks had hollowed noticeably
and your hind legs moved less nimbly
but eyes closed, your face lifted eagerly
to the receding winter sun,
and your nose cast about for all the familiar scents.

You were fading like the mild January afternoon
that had beckoned you outside one final time
to sniff the pungent rosemary in early bloom—
your last curious foray into your jungle yard.

CPSIA information can be obtained
at www.ICGtesting.com
Printed in the USA
BVHW071944070719
552809BV00001B/314/P